I AM
Q.U.E.E.N

Isha R Akinsete

Printed in the United Kingdom

Copyright © 2021 Isha Akinsete

Produced by Bytels Publishing.

DEDICATION

I am Q.U.E.E.N is a daily manifestation guide dedicated to all girls and women.

My hope is that it will help them to see their worth, find their purpose and never settle for less.

TABLE OF CONTENTS

FOREWORD

To rule as Queen, you have to know and believe that you are a Queen, understanding that you don't have to be born into royalty physically to be called or crowned a Queen. I believe many women who have survived struggles and overcome life's toughest battles desire a crown as a Queen. Any woman or young girl who ever feels like they don't deserve the best out of life in my eyes is a Queen, who is fully worth every good thing life has to offer. You deserve to never settle for anything less. Don't believe the lies others have told you, or the insecurities that's imposed on you from society or life in general; you are worthy of every amazing joy and happiness life has to offer.

This amazing book I AM QUEEN is going to take you on a self-love, self -discovery journey, one where loving yourself is your number one priority. Not just loving you but acting out this self-love to help improve your self-development and self-discovery and build self-growth through the power of affirmations and manifestations.

One night I cried my eyes out for three hours. I hated life, hated my journey and hated who I had become due to the pressure of life. I felt like a failure, that everything was a failure, and my choices in relationship and life made me feel like I had failed. All I worked so hard to build felt like it was falling apart. My career I love so much felt like a chore. I was in a very low state of mind. It got to a stage I started regretting all the good things I stepped out into the world to do. I cried and no one came to my rescue. In that moment, after hours of self-pity, it dawned on me that I needed to discover myself, love myself more , start seeing my own self-worth. Many of us Queens look for others to give us what they can't even give themselves. Yes you might have given your all to a relationship, friendship, your career, family and the list is endless, but if you don't give more love to yourself it's all going to come crashing down. You need to daily start pouring love into yourself , saying words to yourself that help develop self-love , self-contentment and build self –wealth, health, self-worth and value. I'm happy to share this amazing book with you. I am convinced it is going to change your life and help you find true self -love and growth.

INTRODUCTION

The power of manifesting the life you want cannot be accomplished until you first decide what you want, your only role today is to decide what you want Queen. Before you can walk into purposeful achievement and abundance you must first know what it looks like to you, figuring out what you know or believe that would make you happy. When making the decision, it must be honest and true to you, true to humanity; it's a decision only you can make. Take a few moments as you decide, write it down onto your vision board, in your planner, diary or journal. However, you do it, you must write it down. In order to see your vision come into full manifestation you must first visualise it in your mind and heart, then move unto writing it down. Make it so clear you can see it daily, believe it is possible for you and that you deserve it, welcome your vision into your life with love and great expectations. Then you can move into the true ways of daily activating the life you desire so much.

Remember, "Manifestation" is a spiritual term. Manifesting something means that something is clear or evident to your mind's eye "you see it and you believe it" and you draw that clear experience into reality with your life attractions. Your life force is determined by those thoughts, actions, and feelings you experience regularly. In order for these affirmations to boost your manifestation, you need to use them daily. Journaling and meditation are great ways to use affirmations repetitively. Practice your healthy, happy thoughts and prepare your mind and spirit to receive your heart's desires.

DAY 1

SELF-LOVE

Self-love is a massively important concept for anyone who's on a path of personal development. If you don't truly LOVE yourself, you're never going to be happy. To create the life you want, you need to be conscious; it requires you to have the confidence to dream big in every area of your life. It requires you to have the ability to decide on what you want, to go after it and to ask for help. It requires you to believe in your dream and your ability to actually make all your dreams come true.

Yes Queen- You;

Yes I am talking to you, you in the mirror, look at your beautiful eyes that tell a million stories, yes I know you might have cried a million tears, but it doesn't matter today. Today you look life in the eyes and you smile, you are beautiful, especially your lips which speak words of kindness on to yourself, words like "I am Queen today and always", and words like

"I am kind, special, intelligent, healthy and wealthy, I am her and she is me. Nothing has the power over me today.

Affirmation:

Yes I am Queen and winning.

I love myself

I am proud of myself

I am doing the best I can

I am enough

I am loved

I am Queen

Write down 3 things you Love about yourself

1. _____

   _____

2. _____

   _____

3. _____

   _____

DAY2

FORGIVENESS

It takes serious effort to truly and completely forgive your own flaws and imperfections, get over your past mistakes and let go of the time that was wasted on self-rage, self -pity and regret. For me arriving at this point has taken a very long time. Living in regret and wishing away the past, constantly saying things like I should have, I could have, carrying this burden every day, and looking back with regret was not a smart choice. Sometimes we say things like I should have taken that opportunity or I should have stayed in that relationship or perhaps I should have left the relationship, I should have moved to that state or country, all the should have, would have, could haves, is too much regret. It's also too much of a burden to bear and sometimes we don't realise how this weighs us down and affects us daily as we go through our lives. Getting to a place of no longer wishing to feel the guilt of your past is so necessary. It's important to realise your mistakes, accept that it's in the past and that you do not have the ability or power to go back in the past and change it. Understand that all you have is now and that your future is what is most important.

It's also necessary to focus on that future you would love to create for yourself. Understand that your past is also a place in your memory, the past mistakes were necessary to shape your future. So often when we find ourselves in a negative situation the first thing we do is to use our thoughts and start to doubt and have regrets. I truly believe that everything that has ever happened in my life was for a reason. I look back at my past mistakes and regrets as a stepping stone for the next level of my life. I have had to develop the mind-set and tell myself daily that I am proud of **me** good or bad, whatever the outcome and that everything that has happened good or bad is working out for my greater good. I have had to strategically write down the affirmations that I would love for you to repeat which is below. Say these words with all your heart and your mind and watch as your life becomes transformed. Today is a good day, embrace it and live. Life happens daily, and we have one chance to react in that moment.

That reaction sweeps off other events, but we managed the best we could in the situation. Now that the situation is over, and you are here in this moment, why carry the burden to eternity when you can drop it by forgiving yourself today. Forgiving yourself is also giving yourself permission to forgive others but first you must learn to forgive yourself daily. Remember that no one is perfect and we are all learning. We are all learning daily, working towards some type of perfection. But even so, in that moment when you do get there, you'll realise that nothing is perfect. The main goal and aim in life is to be grateful and to just live each day as it comes and become the best person you can be for yourself and for everyone around you.

Today is a good day to forgive myself yes, You Queen forgive yourself for putting up with things in the past that you didn't deserve, nobody owes you anything Queen.

So what if you give love and get nothing in return, that was yesterday, last week, last year.

Let it go, the power of forgiveness is necessary for your growth. Forgiveness is the intentional and voluntary process by which one who may initially feel "victimized," undergoes a change in feelings and attitude regarding a given offense, and overcomes negative emotions such as resentment and vengeance.

Therefore Queen you are no longer a victim you are victorious.

Say these affirmations with power and conviction:

Today I walk into my happy place, a place where Love is my light; yes I am Love and Light.

Everyone and everything my light comes into contact with is going to show me love, not fake love but genuine love. Not selfish love, but pure love.

I forgive the past and I set myself free to love and to receive abundant love.

I no longer want to live in the past, I am looking ahead; this is my day.

Now and forever I love myself with all of me.

I forgive myself

I love myself

I am proud of myself

Write down 3 situations or persons you want to forgive

1. _____

   _____

2. _____

   _____

3. _____

   _____

DAY 3

SELF-AFFIRMATION

I often used to try to always please others. There is nothing wrong with doing good, but when you keep doing good, and that comes back to intentionally hurt you, this is not the kind of response a person should be attracting. Getting to a place of not expecting anything in return is the biggest and the best thing you can offer to yourself. I'm sure you have encountered many things being done or said about you and in many cases it's from people you have helped or done a good deed for. Knowing that what's been said about you doesn't have the power over your life means that good or bad what others think about you is none of your business. How they perceive you are is not how you should perceive yourself. You are your number one priority; it is vital that you put your needs first before anything or anyone else. I know it sounds very selfish but you must love yourself first in order to have the power and ability to love others. I often found out from past interviews with other women that they would list the things that they have done for others but never will they say "I have done this for me" it's always "I did the shopping for the family, I clean the house, I did the chores, I did the laundry, I walked the dog, I played with the kids, I did the homework, I cooked for my husband, I waited for him to get back from work" and the list is endless.

So many women that I have met, have put the needs of others before themselves and its quite heart breaking (I'm not saying that you are not loved or others are not appreciating your efforts). However, while you're doing all these things for everyone around you, you must also do things for yourself. Develop yourself, educate yourself, work on yourself, your physical appearance, your health and mental wellbeing, it's paramount. Putting yourself first does not mean that you are neglecting your family, friends or anyone else around you. Putting yourself first simply means that you are choosing to love yourself and being good to yourself in order to feel the love you deserve.

Once others sees that you are able to love yourself and put yourself first they will begin to treat you differently, they will see you for what you're worth and they will deliver that love back to you in return. You will find that they will do things for you rather than you keep doing for them and that's how life should be it should be give and take, not give and give and not receive. Queen listen to yourself, your inner voice; your words and what you think of yourself are what truly matters. How you see yourself how you perceive yourself, how you love yourself, how you believe in yourself is what truly matters in life. Many people are very insecure and this is because they have not practised enough self-love. It's so necessary for us to share narratives like these, read more books about self -love and spend more time alone, get to know ourselves especially before getting into relationships or marriages. Whenever given the opportunity, I like to encourage young girls to get to know themselves before giving themselves to others or before getting into a relationship with men. Once you know the value of something and its worth you will treat it appropriately. Never sell yourself short to please others; never put the needs and the wants of others before your own needs and your wants. Speak positive words over yourself have hope and believe in yourself that you deserve every good thing that life has to offer you, that you are worthy of these things. Use powerful words like the words I've listed below. Stay 'lit' Queen your power is in your words.

Today use your Power words:

Today I reshape my mind with my own words.

Today I am powerful in my purpose

Everything is working for my good this day.

I lack nothing this day.

Write down 3 things you want to do for yourself

1. _____

   _____

2. _____

   _____

3. _____

   _____

DAY 4

GRATITUDE

Comparing your life and competing with the next person is so unnecessary. Competing will steal your happiness and joy. It will steal your focus and distract you from seeing your blessings and purpose. Not comparing or competing is easier said than done because of the world we live in today. When I was a little girl I would cry to my mother and throw tantrums because I wanted what my friends had as many children do today. One day, I was told a parable "take what life has given and wait patiently for what you want" and so over the years Queens, I have learnt to take what life has given to me in the moment but still setting visual goals for what I want in the future. I have learnt to stay grateful in the moment. Queens learn to be happy and content with what you already have in your life. Appreciate life and have fun. Positive thoughts and feelings attract more positivity.

Yes Queen, you are amazing, you have everything you need in this moment; you lack nothing. Today you are a blessing to yourself and anyone who comes into contact with you. Today nothing can stop you from feeling blessed.

Saying the following daily will help you to have a heart of gratitude and contentment:

I am pleased with my days and the experiences that I have!

I have feelings of gratitude and happiness in me!

I have positive emotions in me!

I feel happy and grateful!

I feel content with my life!

I feel happy with my life!

Whatever it is that I do,

I tend to stay pleased! Whatever experiences I have,

I tend to like them and stay content!

My life reveals in joy and harmony!

My life reveals with lots of blessings!

I live a fine, calm, blessed life;

I feel happy, joyous and content!

Write down 3 things you are grateful for in your life.

1. _____

_____

2. _____

_____

3. _____

_____

DAY 5

SELF-ACHIEVEMENT

You owe it to yourself to be happy as much as anyone in the entire universe; you deserve your love and affection. Wanting to be someone else is a waste of the person you are. Accept everything about yourself, I mean everything. You are you, and that is the beginning and the end, no apologies, no regrets.

I was once told I always want what I can't have, I honestly believe that if it exists and it's an honest thing that will benefit my life and the life of others then I can have it. Yes Queen, and so can you, if you ask it shall be given. Queen today ask for abundance, today ask for prosperity, today ask for good health, today ask for love, today ask for whatever your heart so desires and watch it manifest.

Repeat these powerful affirmations

I am worthy of what I desire.

I have everything I need to be successful.

I am grateful for the positive things in my life.

I am open to limitless possibilities.

I achieve whatever I set my mind to.

I am smart, capable and talented.

I believe in myself.

Write down 3 things you would like to achieve.

1. _____

_____

2. _____

_____

3. _____

_____

DAY 6

PROUD MOMENTS

Often in the past, like most women battle with purpose, I was too afraid to step out and share anything with anyone. I just wanted to live life quietly; I never wanted people to know about my life in general. This predominantly is a selfish way to live, why hide your gifts from the world? It's not meant just for you to possess but for you to give to others that's why it's a gift. You were created to rule in your lane, not trying so hard to be the person next door but to take ownership of your purpose. Own it, love it, want it, yes Queen own your lane today and always. Walk in your lane, today be proud of your purpose.

Repeat these affirmations:

I am most proud of myself

I am ready to share my gifts with the world.

I surrender to the wisdom of the Universe.

I am my best source of motivation.

I am creative and open to new solutions.

I choose to embrace the mystery of life.

I choose faith over fear.

I own my life and its purpose

I am grateful for my gifts and abilities

I am ready and willing to share my gifts.

Write down 3 things about yourself you are proud of.

1. _____

   _____

2. _____

   _____

3. _____

   _____

DAY 7

GOAL MANIFESTING

Manifesting the life you want cannot be accomplished until you first decide what you want, and secondly writing it down. Your only role today is to find a quiet place in your home for a few minutes and meditate on what you want Queen. Before you can walk into purposeful achievement and abundance you must first believe with all of your heart. Understand what it looks like to you, what you know or believe that would bring you peace, then, make that decision to go after it. It must be honest and true to you, true to humanity, just and fair. Take a few moments as you close your eyes call it into your space within your mind. See it, visualise it, plan and simply watch your written plans come into manifestation. For the next twenty four hours meditate on what you have visualised and written down, creating a clearer picture in your mind and speak your written goals out loud, keep speaking it out Queens.

Repeat these affirmations:

I go after my goals today

I allow everything to be as it is.

I attract miracles into my life.

I am open to receiving unexpected opportunities.

Write down 3 things you want to see happen in your life.

1. _____

   _____

2. _____

   _____

3. _____

   _____

DAY 8

GENERATIONAL WEALTH

I was so broke and broken at one point in life, I got so tired of living from one pay check to the next. I knew deep down it wasn't the life I wanted to live, and so I dedicated myself to waking up at 5AM every day to speak these words which have changed my life; I am no longer broke. Queens before you speak these words of affirmation make sure you are ready to see it to the end. I assure you these words will change your financial situation and your mental health but you must want it for yourself. You must believe it will work and you must do the work for yourself. The good book says faith without works is dead so you must have faith in your words and apply the work. When you are ready, take deep breaths and breathe out before speaking these words.

Now say the words below like you truly mean it Queens:

I am a Queen

I am a money magnet

I know and believe money flows freely to me.

Today I release all resistance to attracting money into my life

There is always more than enough money in my life now and always

I naturally attract good fortune.

I am financially free and wealthy.

I know my income exceeds my expenses.

I move from poverty mentality to an abundance mind-set.

I am walking in abundance daily.

Write down 3 big things you need to build with money.

1. _____

   _____

2. _____

   _____

3. _____

   _____

DAY 9

GROWING WEALTH

This "I don't deserve it", or "I'm not worthy of it" premise about money is the foundation of self-limiting beliefs that keeps you hostage to your financial situation, and it's not the only one. I have coached several through these self-limiting beliefs, and you know the most shocking part? They don't have the awareness to recognise how their thoughts ruin their finances and destroy their chances of making a lot of money. You have the power to make money Queens, but you must know that money can't make you happy but it has the ability to solve some issues in life.

To attract money speak it into existence:

I am grateful for money.

I love money because money loves me.

I believe there is enough money for everyone.

I attract money to me easily and effortlessly.

I always have enough money.

I am a money magnet.

I make money easily.

I am generous with my money.

I change the world with my money.

I am worthy of the wealth I desire.

I love to give money a good home.

I am open to receiving what is in the highest and best for me

I am open to giving what is in the highest and best for all.

I release all resistance to attracting money

I am financially freedom.

Write down 3 big dreams you need money for.

1. _____

_____

2. _____

_____

3. _____

_____

DAY 10

SELF-DISCOVERY

Before my self-discovery to success, I often thought I wasn't good enough for a life of abundant success. Every time I would achieve something good, I would somehow self-sabotage it. Success wasn't natural to me I often thought that it only happens to people who come from wealthy backgrounds. I would have big dreams of achieving something or becoming something but it would seem so far-fetched because I was unable to see it or imagine it for myself. However as I grew and went through so many life challenges, I refused to settle for less. I started changing my thinking and my belief and even though I didn't see anyone around me on the levels that I wanted to be, I still envisioned myself there. I've always desired to live a purpose driven life and one that inspires others and I eventually realised that success wasn't just about achieving material things but it was also about the impact that you can make with your past experience sharing your narrative and empowering others. 1 learnt to develop an abundance mind-set through the many struggles, I had to change my mind-set completely, telling myself I am good enough to receive abundance and success.

I told myself these very words day and night:

I am worthy of what I desire.

I have everything I need to be successful.

I am grateful for the positive things in my life.

I am open to limitless possibilities.

I achieve whatever I set my mind to.

I am smart, capable and talented.

I believe in myself.

I am my best source of motivation.

I am creative and open to new solutions.

I have faith and I am not afraid.

I attract miracles into my life.

I am open to receiving unexpected opportunities.

I am aligned with my purpose.

I am worthy of positive changes in my life.

I am grateful for the abundance that I have and the abundance that's on its way.

Write down 3 things new things you would like to discover about yourself.

1. _____

   _____

2. _____

   _____

3. _____

   _____

DAY 11

BOUNDARIES

It doesn't take much to knock one's self-confidence. Like many of you Queens, I have had my heart broken over and over I have felt the pain of love breaking my heart, making promises and never living up to them. I have had people in my life who pretended to be friends only to turn around and stab me in the back. Many challenges that have happened in the past can really knock our mental state and ability to try again. And as I went on a self-discovery I was able to see that it wasn't because I wasn't good enough or I never tried in relationships or friendships. It wasn't because I never made an effort it wasn't because I was perfect or unperfected. In many cases we have all tried and given our very best but for some reason life happens and things didn't go the way we would like it to and in the end discouragement stepped in. This then knocked our confidence and desire to try again. You must understand that you have no control over others and how they treat you. You do not have the ability or the power to make a relationship or a friendship work. You as an individual can only try your best and set boundaries for yourself.

When there are boundaries in place you must not change those boundaries or amend your value for anyone. I had to learn the hard way and I know that setting boundaries in my life is necessary. When there are boundaries in place whether it is a friendship or a relationship, the person involved in your life or people involved in your life have to respect your boundaries. In everything in life I've learned that we are bound by boundaries even when taking on a new job. Have you ever been on a job interview, and they told you what the rules are? Once you've taken on that job, they set the boundaries right from your interview and they let you know that if you cross those boundaries you will be out of a job. I believe the same rules still apply in relationship and friendship; it's necessary and crucial that you set clear boundaries from the beginning of any friendship or relationship. Setting boundaries for yourself does not make you better than the person you're in the relationship or friendship with. It just means that you respect yourself and you know what you want and what you deserve from the beginning of any friendship or relationship. Clear boundaries will let that individual know that you are not going to settle for less that your worth in the within the relationship or friendship. You would have control over yourself and how you treat yourself in every situation. You must not set high expectations for others. Keep taking care of your inner peace by speaking good things over yourself.

In the past I have been in relationships and friendships and even in a job without setting clear boundaries for myself and all that did for me was set me up for disappointment heartbreak and setbacks. This is because I entered into such situations not knowing what I wanted; I just wanted something. I wanted a job, I just wanted to feel loved; I just wanted to be friends with someone. It's not until I spent time with myself and discovered who I truly was, and what I want for my life that I changed my mind-set and started putting boundaries in place. There is absolutely nothing wrong with wanting the best for yourself it is your life, and your life is your responsibility. If you leave your life in the hands of others they will mistreat it. They will not see your worth or your value you must take control of your life, you must take control of your decisions, you must choose wisely and set boundaries for yourself.

Do not be afraid to walk away from anything or any situation that no longer serves you or does not respect your boundaries. Life will only give you what you tolerate and what you accept; life is waiting for you to set boundaries for yourself to make the demands for you to choose yourself. Power is never ever given to anyone freely we have to work for it and we have to demand it out of life. I've always said life does not give you what you deserve it gives you what you demand. If you demand respect, respect will be given to you, if you demand love it will be given to you, but you must be prepared to also give this in return. Once you self -discover and know your worth and value; do not ever sell yourself short of what you're worth. Never degrade yourself just because you want to be accepted, love or respected because once you do this it's only temporary. Long term love and respect comes from standing up for yourself setting clear boundaries knowing your worth and never settling.

You must first learn to love yourself, you must first learn to accept yourself, you must learn to want better things for yourself and desire a life that is based on truth and honesty before entering into relationships or friendships or even a career. Never go into any situation such as friendship, relationship, job without knowing what you want out of it. Don't just have something for having it, have it because it add values to your life and it increases your worth, it serves your purpose and builds your future. These are the things you need to consider before entering any type of situations and I'm not saying by doing these things you will not face challenges in fact you probably will face the most challenge because you decide to have a life that is purpose driven. But with every challenge come victory, strength, and more growth. Do not back down from challenges, know that you are built for it, you are created for it and there is nothing you cannot achieve when you love yourself and you set boundaries for yourself.

Say the following like you mean it.

I am worthy of love.

I am capable of loving myself.

I am grateful for my body because…

I am confident in my own skin.

I am compassionate with others and myself.

I attract loving and positive people into my life.

I am strong, brave, and confident.

I am more than my mistakes.

I am proud of myself and all that I have accomplished.

I am a beautiful person, inside and out.

I am worthy of compassion and empathy.

I choose happiness.

I am proud of the person I am and the person I'm becoming.

I am at peace with who I am.

I am aligned with the energy of love.

I am centred, peaceful and grounded.

I have boundaries in my life

I am authentic, true and graceful.

I deserve love, respect, and empathy.

Write down 3 areas you need to set boundaries in your life.

1. _____

_____

2. _____

_____

3. _____

_____

DAY 12

MANIFESTATION OF YOUR DREAMS

Perhaps you might have had a tough time dealing with life and its many challenges. I am sure you have had many thoughts of wanting to give up on your dreams and aspirations. I am sure thoughts of impossibility crept in and made you feel like you were not good enough to accomplish such a task. A few months before I published this book I was faced with one of the biggest property projects I have ever taken on. At the start of the project it seemed so impossible, the thought of "who do you think you are"? And "you know you are not good enough", disturbed my mind for weeks and eventually turned into months of waiting. I eventually got to the place of asking myself "what have you got to lose if you try"? I kept speaking words of confirmations even before seeing the result, I took leaps of faith, I started buying things I wanted to see in the property; I imagined myself on the day of completion. When you are not sure of how or when your dreams will come true you must not give up, instead take a leap of faith and speak it, act it into existence until you see result. Take a moment to think of the biggest thing you think is impossible to accomplish. Then write it down and speak it over your life every day until you see it happen. Act it out in your mind, take a leap of faith. If it's a house you want, get something you would use in the new house, if it's a relationship speak to yourself how you would like to be spoken to in the relationship, if it's a new job dress up for the new job, keep acting all your dreams out into existence.

Say these words to yourself:

I have all that I need to make my life great

I am worthy enough to follow my dreams and manifest my desires.

Everything is working out for my good

I am prepared for what I desire

I continue to climb higher; there are no limits to what I can achieve.

I work hard today to make all of my tomorrows amazing.

Write down 3 things you want to see manifest in the present tense.

1. _____

_____

2. _____

_____

3. _____

_____

DAY 13

RELEASING ANGER

I have learned never to act on my emotions, essentially acting out of a place of anger, pain or sadness. Like so many, struggling to control our anger or express it in a more positive way can be a task. Being anxious for nothing but in everything praying and making your request known to God is important in these circumstances. In many cases, it's easier said than done. When I was younger I struggled to express my anger and frustrations in a calm and constructive way. Today I rarely act out my anger in a negative way. And don't get me wrong, I still get angry, but I know how to control it. Being conscious of your anger issues is the first step in changing. At first, it may feel unnatural to choose to act in a different way, but believe me, you will feel happier and more at peace when you take control of your anger and vent it in a more constructive way. The next step is taking action to improve yourself so you act in a more calm, peaceful and loving way.

Whenever I find myself getting to a place of anger, I repeat the words below to myself

Now say these words:

I can breathe, I am alive, I am thankful

I can feel my anger and I am in control.

I am at peace and harmony with everyone and everything.

I can do better today.

I release all my embodied anger

I remember to stop, relax and think before I act.

I clear and release all my angry thoughts and feelings!

I am too blessed to be angry

I have better things to do with my time than to vent on negative energy; not today.

I choose my inner peace.

Write down 3 things that make you angry and why.

1. _____

   _____

2. _____

   _____

3. _____

   _____

DAY 14

NO LIMITS

Don't limit your life by your current situation; Life has more for you than what you are experiencing. Limitations only exist if you impose them upon yourself within your mind. Free your imagination and let it go in a positive direction. Create your reality, keep showing up as your higher self, every day.

Free yourself of limiting beliefs. Although family and society impressed their beliefs on us as children, you have the final say over what you believe as an adult.

Repeat these affirmations:

I am free of limiting beliefs

I know that my beliefs can drive my behaviour

I nurture my self-esteem

I know that I can achieve greatness just by being myself

I am confident because I know my strengths.

I don't listen to limiting mind-sets

I focus on the plan, not the problem

I do what I have always done,

I will get what I have always desired

I change the way I look at things

I know the things I look at are changing for the better
I am not and will never be limited by others.

I believe in myself and my ability to succeed.

Write down 3 things you need to take the limits off

1. _____

   _____

2. _____

   _____

3. _____

   _____

DAY 15

TIME MANAGEMENT

Life has a way of teaching us the value of time, stop wasting your precious time on things that are not relevant to your peace. As you enter into this new season, value your time and that of everyone around. Your time is your life and if you have no value for your time it means you don't value your life. If every day you put time into your self-growth, you would be on much higher level of growth. Tomorrow is never promised so whatever you invest your time in will be the topic when you are no more. I have had to make some serious life changes when it comes to my time and who I choose to spend it with. The legacy I want to leave behind will determine the choices I make with my time, the people I choose to give my time to, is important. My mother always says if you sleep with duck you are going to quickly quack like a duck. I never want to waste my time with friendships or relationships that are time wasters. I have met so many Queens who have invested into a relationship only to find out their time was wasted by another. Queens your time is your life, build purpose-driven relationships that would lead to a purposeful future. Yes love in everything is the end goal but what's love without a purpose.

Say these power words daily:

Today I will not waste my time

I no longer attract time wasters

I am not a time waster

I add value to the space I am in

I attach valuable achievements into my life

I choose to spend my time on my purpose

I choose to be a purpose builder

I am giving my time to people that see and appreciate my worth.

I de-activate my life from anything or anyone who wants to waste my life.

I am protected and my time is precious

I attract the right kind of energy and people daily.

Write down 3 new ways you can manage your time better.

1. _____

_____

2. _____

_____

3. _____

_____

DAY 16

CREATING PEACE

PEACE is a stress-free state of security and calmness that comes when there's no fighting or war, everything coexisting in perfect harmony and freedom. When you feel at peace within yourself you are content to be the person you are, flaws and everything. Daily choosing peace over chaos is something I had to learn first-hand. I have control of how I feel and how I react in every situation. Gratitude is one way to help with your peace. Being grateful is so powerful and can lift you out of the darkest of times. Be generous especially when you don't feel like it; give back to life. Find someone you can do a simple act of kindness for. It doesn't have to be big. Something as little as opening a door for someone can give a lot of love. Stay connected to your higher power. God is a wealth of comfort for all of us. Reach out and connect as often as you can. The more you do it the more powerful it becomes.

Live in the moment and stop looking into the future at what you want next. Enjoy what is happening now, yes, there's always something you can find right now to appreciate. Make it a habit to always look around and enjoy simple things in the moment like the weather.

Say these affirmations today:

My mind is quiet and stress free.

My body feels calm and light.

I am at peace with myself and the world around me.

Nothing stands in my way of feeling calm and at peace.

Life is beautiful and calm.

My breath is slow and relaxed.

Write down 3 things you can do so to create more peace in your life.

1. _____

   _____

2. _____

   _____

3. _____

   _____

DAY 17

SELF- MEDITATION

Calmness in the midst of chaos is a sign of emotional maturity, stay calm, focused and fabulous Queens. Over the years I've learned that not every situation I find myself being challenged in needs me to respond verbally. I've learnt to pick my battles over the years, I've learnt to master my anger and frustration and stay calm. I've learned to take a million steps back sit down and think before acting. I've learnt to ask myself questions like "is this person worth my time or energy to respond or reply"? I've found out that a lot of situations in life come to test our character, they come to shape us and if we allow our anger and frustration to get the best of us we find ourselves in situations where we end up looking like the bad guy in the end. Not only do we look like the bad guy but we end up feeling 10 times worse than how we felt when the situation happened before we responded. Like many of you Queens, I have been in relationships which tested my character to the fullest and instead of staying calm, and thinking with my head and not my heart, I allowed my emotions to get the best of me. And we all know what happens when your emotions turn from love into anger; it turns into hate and hate fuels aggression. I have learned that many challenges in life that I have faced kept repeating themselves because of how I acted. There's a saying "let your actions speaks louder than your words" it doesn't necessarily mean that you should act out or scream or shout or break things around you when you're upset. It simply means that you set boundaries for yourself, you forgive the person, you stay calm, and you think of another way to react if you must react, or simply just walk away from that thing that no longer serves you. Just simply walk away from that friendship or relationship that no longer serves you. If all it does is drain you, break you, degrade you, and knock your confidence, just simply walk away.

I know it's easier said than done, we've seen so many women around us suffer in silence and our generation of women today feel like they need to voice out their suffering which I absolutely agree with. More women need to speak up, but choose how you want to speak up. You don't necessarily need to stand outside your front door and scream at that person it doesn't change anything. In fact it gives that person the attention and makes them feel like they are so much more important. But if you walk away and choose another way to fight your battle not only will you get attention from that individual but you will also share your experience with another woman who can learn from you. I am never the one to suffer in silence I have always been taught to speak up and say how I feel but over the years, I have chosen how to speak up, when to speak up, and why there's need to speak up. Not every situation deserves your attention and I've also learnt that some situation help to shape your growth and character and shape you into a better person and this may be the reason why you have faced it over and over.

These words will help:

Everything is well in this moment.

I am calm and relaxed right now.

My life is at peace in this moment.

I am surrounded by good and supportive people in my life.

Around me there is an endless pool of peace, harmony and calmness.

I am completely relaxed, calm and safe in this moment.

Right now, everything works perfectly for me.

Life is lovely, and I trust the world to help me live a memorable life.

I am enough.

With every air that I exhale, I release tension.

Every passing day, I feel more relaxed and calmer.

I'll contribute immensely to work.

Just like before, I'll survive this situation.

Take 30 minutes out of your day to meditate, relax and write down 3 things that help you to unwind.

1. _____

_____

2. _____

_____

3. _____

_____

DAY 18

EMBRACING CHANGE

I believe that everything happens for a reason. People change so that you can learn to let go, things go wrong so that you appreciate them when they're right, you believe lies so you eventually learn to trust no one but yourself, and sometimes good things fall apart so better things can come. Knowing life is constantly changing, and people and situations change every day is important. Having control over one's self is paramount. Taking control over your mind and what you allow to affect you daily is necessary. I had to constantly remind myself with words of affirmations and protect my inner peace.

Trust in your inner self Queens and the wider world around you. Free yourself from fear and self-imposed emotional and mental chains.

Affirmation

Today is a good day.

I believe everything happens for a reason

I have no control over others and what they think or do.

I am confident that everything is working out for my good.

I am not afraid of change

I free my mind from chains of worry.

I am clam, free and happy.

Write down 3 new changes you need to embrace.

1. _____
   _____

2. _____
   _____

3. _____
   _____

DAY 19

LETTING GO
OF THE PAST

In a world full of so much darkness you are light, full of love; don't be afraid of the darkness just keep shining. I love the scriptures that says let your life shine before men and give glory to your father who is in heaven, it is one of the scriptures that has shaped my life up until this point. I have faced many challenges in the past which I've spoken out about in my book 'Finding The Balance' and some might think that I've written that book and my challenges have somewhat disappeared. However, ever since publishing that book I will say to you that I have faced many more challenges, some of them seem so unbelievable and yet unexplainable.

Life challenges sometimes can make you feel like giving up or not even wanting to try anymore.

We have seen in our society today that mental health issues has become a headline topic and it is one of the things that I have battled with in the past. Life can be so overwhelming that it affects your mental state it affects your ability to live from day to day and to see the joy or meaning in life. It is very important to not change who you are because of your life circumstance. If you find yourself in a situation which has affected your mental state, well-being and your emotions take yourself out of that situation the best way you know how and put yourself first. Never put a situation or a person or a thing before you; this means no job, nor relationship or friendship, should come before yourself and your mental health. A lot of times people think that health issues relates to physical health only when 100% of the time it comes from mental health issues such as depression, anxiety and these things happen due to life challenges when people are unable to cope with certain situations. Having looked back at many people's lives, and my own, I noticed that everyone is built differently not everyone has the ability to cope with family issues or work issues. Even being a person in today's society in general is difficult and can be a very daunting task for many.

Having hope and something to cling to, surrounding yourself with positive people and positive energy is so paramount; it is one of the things I've had to learn to do. Enjoy life more, live more, seek counselling and therapy when needed not being afraid to speak out when something hurts or someone has hurt you, still keeping your standards and values very high not bringing yourself low in order to make others feel comfortable. It is so necessary Queen's to not let situations and the actions of others affect how you live life and how you choose to carry on from the past and how you choose to live for the future. I often see deep meaning in my challenges; now I see them as a way of life here to teach me a lesson. I ask myself what can I learn from this challenge, how can I grow from this, how can I become a better person from this? I've learned to tell myself that whenever I'm facing a difficult challenge it is not going to kill me but it's going to make me stronger. God knew this would happen to me way before it even happened and so I totally surrender to God, and I surrender to the universe. I often say I have no power of my own; God is more powerful than I am and he has the ability to see me through every situation. I say to myself that everything is working out for my good and eventually it does; it always does. Now more than ever, I've never been happier to be myself, to let my light shine in a world that is so full of darkness. I am happy devoted to shining my light into this world and making an impact and serving a purpose that is greater than myself and I urge you Queens to do the same; but before you do that say your affirmation:

Affirmation

I am no longer controlled by my past

I am light, I am love

I can do anything I put my mind to

I have everything I've ever wanted and needed in life

I am prepared to take on new challenges I can handle anything that comes my way.

I totally surrender to God and his ability tell help me

I am grateful for everything I have in this moment

I am dedicated to living a purpose driven life

I am love I am light I am a giver of love and light, I am a receiver of love and light I lack nothing in this moment and in the future God is able to provide all my needs

My life serves a purpose greater than myself I do not put my trust in men or my career. I put my trust in God

I am blessed, my family is blessed, and every one attached to me is blessed

I have learned from my past and I have the ability to handle the future

I will never shutdown or breakdown

I will only breakthrough and overcome

Write down 3 things in the past you need to let go of

1. _____

   _____

2. _____

   _____

3. _____

   _____

DAY 20

SELF- ACKNOWLEDGMENT

I have never met a strong woman who has never been broken. There's something special about Queens who keep overcoming everything that is meant to destroy them. Use that painful situation and turn it into purpose, use those stones as steps and keep going forward; enough of feeling sorry for you. It's not your fault what has happened in the past can't be changed. You can't go back in time and rewrite it, I am sure if you could, you would. The most important thing to understand in life is that we all, whether you're male or female, will face challenges. And with challenges comes strength with every challenge you face comes belief, it gives you hope and it gives you the willingness to want to succeed if you don't give up when challenged. Perhaps you are in a state of mind and you feel like you want to give up because life is so overwhelming or perhaps you're going through a very difficult challenge whether it is personal, professional or financial if you're able to analyse this challenge, you can overcome it. Try to figure out what this challenge is trying to teach you once you get that, you will be fine. I've lived in a fairy tale dream of believing that life should be perfect that's how I started my childhood.

Even though I was going through challenges, I always believed that there's hope, there's 'gonna' be better days ahead. Things will get better and that's how I've literally carried myself through adulthood even though I'm facing challenges. Even if it is the most difficult challenge and I don't see a way out, I always try and see the good in that no matter how difficult it is. Perhaps that's what's helped me to get to this point I am at in my life which I'm truly grateful for. I'm grateful for every challenge I faced, every difficulty that I've overcome I am so grateful for the hard times because it's made me strong it's made me grow it's made me take things out of my life that shouldn't be in my life. It's made me develop an incredible mind-set and made me have a work ethic like no other. I just want you to know that it's okay to have hard challenges or difficult times in life; nothing is perfect and no situation is perfect.

Time is constantly changing and so will you. Yes we all want a fairy tale ending but trust me life is made up of both balancing the good and the bad and somewhere in the middle you eventually find your own happiness. This is what makes you happy and makes you see life worth living. It's so important not to give up until you are able to understand what the life challenge is trying to teach you in that moment. You might be going through a financial situation or relationship situation or a personal/ health situation but if you are able to analyse things and just look at your blessing, balance the outlook based on how blessed you are on one hand and then match that challenge with your blessing and just say to yourself "look I've been through so much on this hand but on this hand life is working out for me in this way. Count your blessings daily and be daily grateful for where you find yourself. There is no way on this earth where there isn't a human being who has got a reason to be grateful or does not have a reason to match their blessing with their challenges in life. We all have something to be grateful for, the fact that you are alive and you are breathing that is enough reason for you to be grateful. One thing I find about challenges especially women who have gone through hard times is that we are able to overcome it Queens! We are able to bounce back and make something out of ourselves. We are able to inspire a generation of other women coming behind us because we did not give up. When I look back into history and all the women that have worked tremendously hard and faced difficult challenges they have done it for our generation so that now, many of us can look in history books and say 'wow', "if they can do it so can I". There is no strong woman without a challenge or problem we all have to face it and in facing this you are able to develop more strength and character. Develop; I hope you develop yourself and you find yourself. As you find yourself you continue to find yourself some more and believe in yourself some more too.

Here are a few words to always remember:

I am strong physically

I am strong mentally

I am strong emotionally

I am strong spiritually

I am strong financially

I have strength for myself

I have strength for my

I have strength for my friends

I am grateful for my strength

I am determined to succeed

Write down 3 things you are most proud of about yourself.

1. _____

   _____

2. _____

   _____

3. _____

   _____

DAY 21

CHANGE

Change comes when you decide that you want change, but most importantly making a conscious decision that you no longer want to remain in the same situation will change your life for the better.

It's all in the mind, if you can change your mind, you can change your whole life. I have realised that any change is good, both good and bad changes, at times it may seem very frustrating trying to adjust to the changes of life trying to figure out which path to take. Life is constantly changing, whether we want it to or not, our life is also changing. Too often people run away from changes because they are afraid to try new things or step out of their comfort zone. In many situations, it's our minds that keep us from moving forward. As a child, I often used to hear a proverb that says " if you keep telling yourself you don't have then you will never have" over the years this stuck with me even when I didn't have enough I would try not to say it to myself. Understanding that your words have the power to create and shape your reality. Learn to change you words, my mother always used to say to me as a child "think before you speak" always think about what you want for yourself first before speaking it onto yourself. If you want a life of abundance, keep speaking abundance over your life, keep your mind focused on that abundant life and it will become your reality.

Say these life changing affirmations

I live a life of abundance

I am grateful for the changes in my life.

I embrace my past and my future

I seek a life of peace and joy

I have an overflow of blessing

I am a blessing to myself and others

I am happy for the positive changes in my life

I am thankful for my abundance in good health and wealth

I attract and embrace changes

I learn and grow from every change in my life

I am capable of changing my life for the better

Write down 3 things you want to see change.

1. _____

   _____

2. _____

   _____

3. _____

   _____

DAY 22

PATIENCE

One of the biggest things I battled with in the past was that I wanted things to be done quickly. I am sure you have also felt frustrated when you know what you want out of life but things are not happening as swiftly as you would like them to, so disappointment steps in and you think it's not going to happen anymore. Queens listen, do not set time frames for things; they will happen when they are meant to. Be content with the knowledge that the universe and God has received your intentions and will work on them when the time is right. Make clear and honest intentions, believe it will happen and let it happen, don't ask questions about when it will happen just believe it will. Set goals but you have no power over time and when things will get done.

Feel at peace with things you do not know or understand. Do not try too hard to understand everything, rather allow yourself to open up to not fully knowing things, and feel comfortable with this situation. Accept things, and you will soon find that the knowledge and understanding finds you, rather than you finding it. Everything will come to you in the right time. You don't have to steal, lie, cheat, or settle for less than who you are just to fit in or fill a void, set yourself apart knowing that your own path has been created for you even before you were born. The life you so much desire is possible and it will come to you at the right time. You don't need to be in a hurry to do anything just let life happen. Set clear boundaries and keep speaking positive words over yourself daily. I also know and believe that life has a way of giving us exactly what we need at the perfect time. We live in a world where Queens are impatient, we live in a world of instant gratification; we don't like waiting for things but some of the most beautiful things in life come out of patience.

Affirmation:

Everything I need already exists

Today I choose patience

I am filled with calm and stillness

I trust that everything will happen in its own time.

The universe will give me everything I desire when it is the right time.

I breathe in love and patience

I feel at ease while waiting

Things are calm and I am drifting happily

I pause to listen

I feel content to wait

I am content with my life.

Write down 3 areas where you need to practice patience

1. _____

_____

2. _____

_____

3. _____

_____

DAY 23

ASK FOR IT

Learning to spend time with one's self will help you to discover new things. You get to see and discover things about yourself you never knew existed. We've all gone through the global pandemic. These times have forced some of us to more self-discovery for example learning that detachment is a good thing. Like many Queens, being alone or breaking off a relationship or friendship that no longer serves a purpose, can be difficult but in the end you grow and develop for the next level of life. Do not attach too much weight to an outcome; you want something, desire it, but do not let yourself feel that you need it. The Law of Attraction states that when you focus on things with enough intent, it will eventually appear. The good book says 'ask and it shall be given' but we must wait patiently, and with a sense of gratitude for what we will receive. You should imagine what you want, visualise having it, act as though you already have it, but then give no attention to the outcome occurring.

Use affirmations to maintain focus, but do not become obsessive.

I am not obsessed over anything or anyone.

I am grateful for all I have

I am thankful for life and health

I am confident in my ability to succeed in life.

I know everything I desire will appear at the right time.

I believe once I ask with good intent I will receive

God knows my needs they will all be met.

Write down 3 things that you want to accomplish with dates.

1. _____

_____

2. _____

_____

3. _____

_____

DAY 24

THE REASONS WHY

Today, know clearly why you want something. This gives you the correct mind-set and willpower to send out the correct requests without conflicting intentions that confuse matters. Your goals must really strike a chord deep within you.

Don't limit your life by your current situation; Life has more for you than what you are experiencing. Limitations only exist if you impose them upon yourself within your mind. Free your imagination into a positive direction and create your reality, keep showing up as your higher self every day.

Affirmation

I am happy with my life today

I know what I want

I believe all my inner most desires are met

I don't believe in limitations

I am soaring to a higher level of positive

I free my imagination into a creative direction

I embrace all life has to offer me.

Write down 3 reasons why you want your goals to be accomplished.

1. _____

_____

2. _____

_____

3. _____

_____

DAY 25

IMPROVEMENT

I believe every woman is capable of being a business woman, a boss in every way. When I was growing up men were the business-minded ones and business owners. Now Queens have taken the front line in business, we are balancing it all with family and still looking amazing. I have never been more proud of the Queens I see today and I know we are capable of so much more. Building generations and generational wealth for our daughters and sons is paramount. I remember I was 12 years old when my mother introduced me to my first side hustle. We had mango trees at the back garden in South America, she said you can sell these mangoes at school and you can make a profit. I remember the first day I ate half of the batch before selling the rest. I soon learnt the art of business is not to eat first but to sell first and make a profit. Know this Queens, you have everything you need to build and successfully run your business. Remember your business is nobody's business it's yours; keep praying over it, working on it, keep speaking words of affirmations over it daily. You are fully capable of making money and balancing your family and yourself. Even when others don't support you believe that nothing is too difficult for you to achieve. Keep marketing yourself, and promoting your brand, invest your time and money into your business. Keep speaking positive affirmations over it daily. Before you go into a new day speak to yourself about what kind of day you want your business to have, and the kind of clients you want to connect with.

Affirmation

I am smart and successful.

My clients enjoy working with me

I am an impactful leader.

I am worthy of financial security.

My business is growing and so am I.

My business is making amazing profits

My life is overflowing with opportunities.

I am turning my expertise into income.

I will honour my journey and free myself from the expectations of others.

I am making a positive impact in the lives of others.

My mistakes do not define me.

I am building generational wealth

I am my own legacy for my family.

Write down 3 things you want to improve with yourself or business.

1. _____

_____

2. _____

_____

3. _____

_____

DAY 26

STEPPING OUT IN FAITH

I remember when I wrote 'Finding The Balance' a few years ago I felt like life was waging war over me, it was a constant battle to survive mentally until I was able to see the pattern in my life. On one hand I would have so many struggles and on the other hand something good would happen and every-time I found peace it seemed unreal. I was constantly thinking about what was around the corner. After I published the book, I saw the difference it made and why I felt like my life was constantly under pressure. When you are loaded with purpose life puts pressure on you to deliver that's why it feels like you are being attacked. It's because of what you have within you Queens, you have so much potential and gifts that life is demanding out of you and know this

'Thieves Don't Break into Empty Houses'. What you're carrying within you is valuable. Keep going and don't give up. Life rarely ever goes exactly as planned. Many times life will take you in a completely different direction to the path you intended to travel.

No matter what happens HAVE FAITH! Don't stop being you, don't stop praying, don't stop affirming and meditating on your purpose. Until you feel free and you help others to be free also.

Affirmation

I create my life on a quantum level. There are endless opportunities.

I have a healthy body, tranquil mind and a vibrant soul.

I am enough.

I don't entertain negativity in any shape or form. I simply let it go.

I love the fact that so many people have faith in me

I create happiness by appreciating the little things in life.

I am blessed to have a wonderful family and friends.

I embrace the rhythm of life and let it unfold.

I focus on action to create the life I want. The smallest step can end years of stagnation.

I know my intuition will always take me in the right direction.

I adore my quirks because they make me unique.

I can become anything I put my mind to.

I believe in my dreams and I won't stop until they become real.

I always give when I can because I know it always comes back.

I see failure as a golden opportunity to learn.

I know that massive action cures everything.

I love the creative energy that flows through me.

I work for my desires because I don't want regret.

I don't live for things I live for a spiritual purpose.

Write down 3 areas you need to step out on Faith.

1. _____

_____

2. _____

_____

3. _____

_____

DAY 27

SPREADING LOVE

There is darkness inside each one of us. In a world full of so much darkness, sometimes the darkness never seems to lighten. We surround ourselves with the dark things of this world and convince ourselves that this is who we are. We forget that there is also an inherent light inside each of us. We forget that darkness is temporary. We forget that all we simply need to do is turn on the light. No matter how dark it may be, if we simply remember to flip the switch, or even light a candle, we can still become a beacon of hope. Even if it is only a beacon for yourself, don't hide your light; keep shining it and sharing it. I have worked with so many amazing Queens in the past who shared their feelings about other women who make them feel less important because of something or someone. I never want to make another woman like me feel less important because of status or any other position. I have seen too often women who will see other women doing well and in instead of supporting, they gather with others to destroy that woman. Forgetting that she is just like you, she is your sister not your enemy. I have experienced first-hand hatred by other women. I have had women pretend to be my friends only to get close enough to stab me in the back. Such situations I no longer entertain in my life. Life is more beautiful when Queens genuinely support and love each other; no competition, no fakes just pure love. Seek to be a Queen that promotes peace instead of hate, I always think of life after death what would I want my family and friends to remember me for? The legacy I want to leave for other Queens like myself is to always remember that we all deserve a seat at the table of life and if one of us wins before the other we are all winners. I daily remind myself with affirmations of peace that I am peace to myself and every Queen who comes into contact with me.

Say these affirmations today:

I am love and light.

I am a builder I support other Queens

I want to see other women winning

I am happy when I see other Queens happy

I genuinely support and clap for others

I am at peace with my own success

I am proud of every Queen I see, I am her and she is me

I am winning when I see other Queens winning

I offer peace and love to the next Queen

I am never in competition with other Queens like myself

I am a vision supporter for other Queens

I am a builder for myself and other Queens

I am a shoulder for other Querns to lean on.

I am my sister's keeper

I am blessed to be a blessing to others.

Write down 3 Queens you need to show your support and love to.

1. _____

_____

2. _____

_____

3. _____

_____

DAY 28

HEALTH

We're told again and again from a young age "nobody's perfect, everyone makes mistakes." But the older you get, the more pressure you feel never to fail. Cut yourself some slack Queens. Make mistakes so you can learn and grow from them. Embrace your past don't run from it or try to cover it up. You're constantly changing and growing from who you once were into who you are today and who you will be one day. So forget about that voice in your head that says you need to be perfect. Make mistakes lots of them. The lessons you'll gain are priceless. Never feel the pressure to compete with anyone. Remember your value doesn't lie in how your body looks or what you put on. So many things in the world want to distract you from this powerful truth. Sometimes even your own internalised sexism affirms your thoughts of inadequacy. You are valuable because you are you, not because of your body shape, size or colour.

So, wear what makes you feel good do what makes you feel happy. If it's a lot or if it's a little, wear what makes you feel confident and comfortable. Exercise daily Queens, take care of your health, be good to your body, go for walks. Be careful what food you put into your body daily not just when you're on a diet, what you eat daily will show on your skin and every other parts of your body.

Affirmation

I love myself and my body

I no longer compare myself to others

I don't worry about others' opinions of me

I allow myself to learn from my mistakes

My value doesn't lie in how my body looks

I am not afraid to let go of toxic people

I allow myself to process all my fears

I trust myself to make good decisions for myself.

I am a magnet for joy

I am a magnet for peace

I am a magnet for health

I am a magnet for abundance

I am a magnet for love

Write down 3 ways you need to take care of your health.

1. _____
   _____

2. _____
   _____

3. _____
   _____

DAY 29

RECEIVING TRUE LOVE

Even if you're feeling content being single, you might be ready for your soulmate or for a lasting, healthy relationship. Manifesting a loving, healthy relationship is completely possible. As Queens, we all desire a perfect love life as much as we may claim we love ourselves and we are happy being single that's fine as long as you're truly happy. It's also vital to share the love with someone special and understand that you are worthy of receiving love. Finding love or should I say love finding you sometimes is not as simple as it seems. We live in a world where fake love is more common that genuine love and because of this so many Queens find it hard to trust love. We have seen other Queens around us and before us who have experienced so much hurt and pain from love for many years and because of this, many Queens have vowed never to love again and never to invest in love. Many Queens have misunderstood the experiences of others in the past and have taken it upon themselves to not let love in. Never forget that everyone's journey is different, it's good to learn from other's mistakes but it's important to not compare your journey with others.

Just because something didn't work out for others doesn't mean it wouldn't work out for you. Life is constantly changing and with life changes people also change. Some Queens have this conception that all men are the same, or all men cheat or all men are dogs and the list is endless. I find when you know and love yourself to a certain degree you build yourself up for love. If I know the worth of something, a bag for example, I might go get a fake copy but within myself I know it's fake, the way I would wear it for example will make others think so too.

Before you manifest the love you want, you must believe that you are worthy of it and that it is real. Your worth is none negotiable; know that you are valuable to any man that finds you. Believe that you carry a special kind of favour within you, that when you do love that person they will have to add value to your life. Know that you are worthy of receiving authentic love and in return, you will be open to love when it comes into your life. Queen before you say you affirmation, you are going to need an envelope, a pen and paper. Write down what you want from the love you desire and draw a line down the page. On the other half of the page, write down how you would love to share your side of love with the person of your desire. For example I would love for my soulmate to be a playful person in return I will pray with my soulmate. Once you have done this, put it into the envelope and close it. When you meet this special some share this with them. If you are already with your soulmate you can still us this exercise daily to keep your attraction to one another fresh.

Here are affirmations to help you on this special journey say it daily.

I give my heart, ready to receive the heart of another.

I am loved more than I ever thought possible.

I am open to receive knock-my-socks off love.

I am making room for an amazing partner in my life!

My partner shows me deep, passionate love.

I am in a wonderful relationship with someone who treats me right!

I deserve love and affection.

I am attracting the perfect person for me.

I love who I am, and so does my partner.

I am worthy of a healthy, loving relationship.

I am open to love.

I am surrounded by love.

I trust the universe to bring my true love to me.

I am in the healthiest relationship of my life!

I allow love to find me

Write down 3 ways you will be open to receiving Love.

1. _____

   _____

2. _____

   _____

3. _____

   _____

MENTAL HEALTH

Taking care of your mental and emotional health is equally as important as taking care of your physical appearance. Never neglect your mental health, more women than ever are now presenting with a common mental disorder, such as depression. 25% of young women between the ages of 16-25 (APMS 2016) report symptoms of common mental disorder (mainly anxiety and depression). Rates of self-harm and suicide in women are higher than ever, again especially in young women. Ever since the global pandemic, many women's mental health has been affected, essentially women who earn a living from the beauty and social media industries. If you are so dependent on anything in life when it's taken away it's extremely difficult to live without it. Making sure that you check in with yourself and others is vital. I have always done a check up on myself daily. I look in the mirror and say "how are you doing Queen, do you need me to do anything for you"? I know it sounds strange but it's necessary to check up on you. Taking a moment to reflect on yourself and your many accomplishments over the years is important. You might think you haven't achieved a lot but the simple fact that you are alive is a big achievement. Stop being so hard on yourself, give yourself some credit even for the little things.

Speaking and spending time with positive friends or family is vital for your mental health, self-care is paramount; it will help to boost your mental health and self-confidence. Some Queens like shopping, while others might like going to the gym and eating healthy. It's important to make time for yourself, daily do one thing for you that you love and enjoy doing. Having a positive mind-set can do wonders for your attitude. Looking at life situations from a different perspective can help you find more creative solutions. Try to seek better health, strive to do better in school or work, in the long run, this will be beneficial to your life and even help you to live longer. When people get into a negative rut or are dealing with depression or anxiety, their self-talk tends to be negative and pessimistic. One way you can combat this tendency is to make time each day to say some positive affirmations. Say it out loud or in your mind, these daily affirmations can improve mental health and turn you into a more optimistic person. Here are the daily affirmations that you can start using today to improve your mental health.

Affirmation

Today I put me first

My mind is in a good place

I am grateful for all I have

Healing is possible for me.

I am enough.

I am not and will never be defined by a diagnosis.

I can challenge my negative thoughts with positive ones.

I am thankful for the positive things and people in my life.

I love myself for who I am.

I love my mind and body.

I am looking at life with a positive mind-set

I can achieve anything I set my mind on.

I care for myself daily.

I am proud of myself.

I am attracting inner peace, love and light.

I only attract healthy relationships.

I am happy to give and receive love every day!

I find love everywhere I go.

I am in a relationship with someone I respect who also respects me.

I am open to a healthy, loving relationship that is right for me.

Love starts with me.

I am love and light.

I naturally find love everywhere.

I am very charismatic.

I am lovable.

The more I love a person, the more they love me in return.

My relationships are always fulfilling.

I am grateful for the love in my life.

Sharing love comes easily to me.

I am attracting real connection.

My heart is prepared to receive love.

I connect with others easily.

I love effortlessly.

Write down 3 things you can do for yourself to improve your mental health

1. _____

_____

2. _____

_____

3. _____

_____

DAY 31

TAKING NOTES

Know this, you are a kingdom daughter, your life is precious in the eyes of God; you are created for greatness. You were born to make a difference in this world. You have a special purpose in life, one that only you can fulfil, I can't be you and you can't be me no matter how hard we try. You alone can play the role of you; no other women can take the place of your distinct purpose. You are not defined by want others think or say about you. Your path from birth is carved out just for your footsteps alone. Your strength and imperfection is perfect for your purpose, you are never too much and you are certainly trying your best at life. So never doubt your ability to achieve anything you set your mind to.

I am not saying it's going to be easy, in fact the more you try to achieve, the more the challenges, but when you push past the challenges you are able to achieve some unimaginable things. Keep striving to develop into the best version of yourself, you don't need access, acceptance or approval to grow and develop, permit yourself to be great and grow. What you tell yourself daily Queen is what will be your voice to keep going when you don't feel like it. Your environment plays a very big part in your growth, I am sure you remember your parents or grandparents saying 'birds of a feather flock together', so it's important to surround yourself with good energy. If you find a relationship or friendship is draining you or stopping you from growth both mental growth and physical growth you must distance yourself from it. Protect your peace at all cost. Your mental health is important in your growth, protecting your inner peace at all costs.

Queens, you need people in your life that are happy for you when you're happy; people who celebrate you when they see you winning in life. You need good vibrations daily to connect to your good energy. If you are struggling with staying positive then take a look at your surrounding energy. For example, you could wake up in a good mood, and suddenly someone calls you and you don't need to answer just seeing the name pop up and your mood just completely changes. You might not have anything against that individual but you can sense the negative energy. Queens learn to follow your gut instinct; it is a way of pre-warming you when something is off. Never forget to meditate daily when using positive affirmations. Pray every time you can as often as you can. Keep your spirit fed with positivity keep reading positive books to help you grow and spread love not to hate to keep your heart as pure as you can. I'm not saying everyone should be perfect but to embrace their imperfection. Don't do things to intentionally hurt others. You should never be responsible for another woman's pain. Make wise choices Queens and keep choosing peace over pain. Love over lose, joy over jealousy, and compassion over competition.

I love you Queen; keep loving yourself and paying it forward for the next Queens to come.

Affirmation

I am fearless

My challenges help me grow

I choose to let go of everything that no longer server me.

I live my life on my own terms.

My life is full of purpose and passion.

All is well within me; I feel safe.

I am free from all worry and anxiety.

I am stronger when I overcome my fears.

I let go of all negative thoughts and beliefs.

I love myself and I am proud of myself.

I choose a life of peace.

I choose love over loss.

I am living in the moment.

I am thankful for everything and everyone in my life.

Write down 3 things that's not promoting your good vibes

1. _____

   _____

2. _____

   _____

3. _____

   _____

Printed in Great Britain
by Amazon

62066337R00061